Rex Preston's
PEAK DISTRICT
AND
PENNINES

Rex W. Preston

HALSGROVE
In association with
GRANBY GALLERY

First published in Great Britain in 2003

British Library Cataloguing-in-Publication Data
A CIP record for this title is available from the British Library

ISBN 1 84114 286 7

HALSGROVE
Halsgrove House
Lower Moor Way
Tiverton, Devon EX16 6SS
Tel: 01884 243242
Fax: 01884 243325
email: sales@halsgrove.com
website: www.halsgrove.com

Printed and bound by D'Auria Industrie Grafiche Spa, Italy

Moorland Sunset, Derbyshire   *20 x 30in   Oil*

Contents

Foreword   5

Interview with Rex Preston   11

Andrew Macara's View   32

Robin Gibbard meets Rex Preston   33

Peak District and Southern Pennines   34

Northern Pennines   120

Waterfalls, Fairbrook, Derbyshire *24 x 30in Oil*

This book is dedicated to Jean Woodward, my late mother-in-law,
without whose initial help and encouragement it would not have been written.

Foreword

by

Michael Mosley – Granby Gallery, Bakewell

'I only had a proper job once and that only lasted three years!' Such is the modesty of Rex Preston. He was referring to his time at Bemrose the printers in Derby, where he was employed as a design artist.

I recall seeing this young man, some twenty years my junior, visiting on a fairly regular basis the various exhibitions we held in our gallery. I must confess I did wonder who he was, because he spoke very little indeed, if

Horse Chestnut Trees, Haddon House Farm
15 x 22in Watercolour

at all, until one day he posed the question, 'Would you be interested in exhibiting a group of my limited edition prints set in oval frames? If you care to look, I have them in my car outside in the car park.' I had previously seen some of Rex's oil paintings, albeit some of his earlier work, and had not been over-enthusiastic, but I was happy to see what was on offer. I decided I would like to stretch my legs, so volunteered to go with him to the car. Rex was calling on his way back from the Hope Valley, where he had been delivering some watercolour drawings to a gallery. For some reason, Rex had missed one that was hidden under a rug and as he moved the prints, this came to light. It was a little jewel! He allowed me to take it and it only stayed on show in the window for twenty-four hours before being sold. I telephoned this new artist in great haste to ask, 'Have you any more watercolours?' Several duly arrived and they sold very quickly so I proposed the idea of a watercolour exhibition. Twelve months later we had a most successful show of Rex Preston's watercolours – a sell-out!

I was a little disappointed when Rex then announced he was going back to painting in oils. However, the discipline of the watercolour medium had influenced the style of his painting, and the rest is history, with people literally queuing in the rain for three hours to get pole position for previews of his oil painting exhibitions at our gallery.

Living on a farm, I had the occasion once to accept the request of an artist, who wanted to explore the fields for subjects to paint. He only found two or three within the whole farm! A couple of years later Rex made the same request. We set off in the same direction with me leading through the first field at a rate of knots, commenting, 'There's nothing in here Rex.' 'Hey, hold on a minute!' he exclaimed. 'Three paintings (all sold) came from that first field alone! So many people will look and not see.'

Rex is a true and dedicated artist who has no desire to be, and will not be, influenced by commercial pressures. He loves the countryside, the different aspects and moods created by light and the weather: a true master in choosing subjects. 'Look, they are all around you,' he will say.

Over the last twenty years or so Rex and I have become firm friends, both understanding what makes the other one tick, and accepting that the difference in our characters and outlooks is the cornerstone of our success together. He gets on with painting and I with running my gallery, neither interfering with the other. Whilst neither of us likes to be told what to do, the word 'commission' has long been removed from our vocabularies. The look on Rex's face if an unsuspecting client should broach the subject of commissions is unbelievable.

This illustrates the man he is. To be asked to paint somebody's house or favourite spot is hardly inspiring for an artist, and surely the inspiration is what it is all about. So if there isn't a picture that suits the client from the selection he presents at an exhibition – bad luck! Rex is fuelled by the strong forces of nature. He will trek for miles wearing his hiking boots to find a suitable subject, and having found it, has been known to wait for the light to change or the weather to abate. This is the measure of the man who can only record on canvas what he feels from his heart, leaving all the popular scenes so frequently painted by others, for them to relish.

It is so then that Rex explores and hikes for miles and miles in pursuit of fresh subjects away from the milling crowds and unseen by the average person such as myself. Whilst these explorations can take him far from Derbyshire to Scotland, the Lakes, Yorkshire Dales, Cornwall and even across to Suffolk, it was a place in Derbyshire frequently painted by Rex that aroused my interest, so, donning my walking boots, I asked him how to get there. 'I will take you,' he volunteered. I (almost) wished I had never asked! The place in question was Fairbrook Valley, a couple of miles from the main Sheffield–Manchester road. Having parked our car near the Snake Inn, we crossed the road and followed a path that had, in all fairness, been made easier to tackle by the good services of the Peak Park authorities, who had scaled the streams and waterways with wooden bridges. For me it was still a fairly hard trek. Any discomfort was, however, totally mitigated by the supreme scenery that we were absorbing. 'How do you like this then?' Rex asked. 'Magnificent,' was my reply. I could appreciate why he was drawn here. 'If we keep going,' he exclaimed, 'we come to Kinder, another area that I like to visit and paint.' This brought back to my mind a 20 x 30in painting that had been reproduced by Solomon & Whitehead as a fine art print entitled 'Evening Light, Kinder', depicting a shepherd seated under Kinder on a boulder, resting with his dog by his side waiting to continue the journey home. This was an incredibly popular print and many have asked for it to be reprinted, but the publishers feel that there are so many other subjects of Rex's that they are doing these instead.

One such is Calton Lees, the only watercolour drawing that has been printed and presented as a signed artist's print. The picture was painted by accident, or at least by a change of circumstances. Rex had decided one February day to leave his home in South Derbyshire and travel to Kinder for a day's sketching. On leaving home all was fine, but when he reached Rowsley on the A6, before turning off for Chatsworth, there was snow. By the time he had reached the park bridge, it was getting serious, so he decided, rather than get stuck, he would park his car by the Chatsworth nurseries and explore. Calton Lees, the small hamlet a little further on, provided this ideal subject.

Snowscene, Calton Lees, Chatsworth   *16 x 30in Watercolour*

As I mentioned previously, Rex does not involve himself with the commercial aspect of his career and I have been privileged to help him with furthering the exposure of his work through greeting cards and fine art prints, the latter in both open and signed limited editions. These have been a great success, with cards on sale through many retailers, including national outlets, and his prints can be seen regularly throughout the country.

Many of Rex's friends have a connection with, or are actually artists, but not all of course. He is a keen keep-fit man and has a good eye for potting the black ball in the snooker rooms, where he also has many friends. It is always a delight, when Rex has an exhibition, to see these people, in addition to family, coming along to support him and share with pride the success and enjoyment of his skills. His family, who mean so much to him, have been a great support over the years. His wife, Sue, is the perfect foil to Rex the artist. In her professional life, she is the office manager at a firm of chartered accountants, and this training allows her to keep watch over the business side. Rex prefers to give his time totally to his painting. He has already declared that this book would not have materialised without the enormous input from Sue, who has diligently recorded his comments on computer.

One of Rex's paintings entitled 'Hey, Wait for Us!' was published as a fine art print many years ago. This featured two young children, a girl and a boy, running excitedly with buckets and spades towards the beach at Woolacombe, North Devon, outpacing their parents, Rex and Sue, who are calling, 'Hey, wait for us!' This was Mark and Michelle, who have since grown up and are both doing well in their chosen fields. Michelle has a degree in nursing and works in a busy A & E department. Mark has followed in his father's footsteps, becoming an up-and-coming artist, with his own style which is creating much interest. He has already held several one-man exhibitions with enormous success.

As well as the memory of our visit to Fairbrook Valley, perhaps my other lasting memory of Rex is a visit to the Constable exhibition in London.

We viewed all the pictures, with Rex commenting to me on how he appreciated them from an artistic viewpoint. The oil sketches, albeit the same size often as the finished painting, were to be admired in their own right. This preliminary approach on canvas by the artist to capture the design, mood and colours of the subject ultimately to be produced, was fascinating. Rex commented that often he preferred the 'sketch' to the finished picture, and I saw and agreed with his point of view.

As you browse through Rex's paintings, you will see several of his sketches, which to me are little treasures. I hope you enjoy the book.

Michael Mosley

Rex sketching at Fairbrook
(Photograph taken by Michael Mosley)

Hey, Wait for Us, Morte Bay, Woolacombe, Devon   *12 x 24in Oil*

Painting on location in Fairbrook Valley

Beginning a snow scene in the studio

Interview with Rex Preston

Where were you brought up?

I was born in Yardley, Birmingham, in July 1948 and lived there until the age of five when my parents became licensees. We moved to a new pub every few years and, together with my sister and two brothers, I lived in Wolverhampton, Coleshill, Warwickshire, and Newcastle-under-Lyme before moving to Derbyshire at the age of almost sixteen.

What stimulated an early interest in painting?

I remember clearly, sitting on my father's knee when I was about three or four and being fascinated by watching him do a colour drawing of a cottage in a landscape.

An art teacher at Orme School for Boys in Newcastle-under-Lyme made an impression on me when he used to regularly stand in front of the class and create a picture on the blackboard in chalk. I was impressed that someone could create a picture from his imagination so effectively just with chalks.

At Newcastle-under-Lyme School of Art, at the age of fifteen, my first lesson with Monty Grainger was truly memorable. He asked us all to paint what we could see out of the window. He then came back into the room, took one look at our work and told us to go upstairs, fill the bath and wash off all that we had done. He then took a sheet of paper, and using only three colours, painted the most stunningly subtle tonal painting. I remember being fascinated by every colour mix and brush stroke. To me that was inspired teaching. We were putting in too much detail; his was brilliant because of its simplicity.

My dad was always busy looking after the cellar or the bar, but I would often paint a picture and take it to him. If his reaction was good, I would feel a great sense of achievement as it didn't happen very often. A very good reaction would make me want to paint an even better one next time. Even now, if he points out one that he particularly likes, I have a closer look; it's not usually the obvious choice.

Do you feel that artistic talent can be inherited?

My father went to art school and before the war worked as a copper plate engraver in Birmingham. I believe my brother Jim and I have both inherited some of his artistic talent so I do think talent is inherited. But its important to have the drive and enthusiasm to make the best use of it.

Are your childhood memories happy or sad?

I have many happy memories of my childhood, but many unhappy ones from my school days.

I particularly enjoyed living in Coleshill for several years from the age of eight. My parents were quite preoccupied with the licence trade and I had a lot of freedom to do as I pleased, spending most of my time with my friends racing around the fields and woods or fishing in the local rivers and ponds. I had more friends in Coleshill as we stayed there longer than most other places.

I particularly remember our family holidays in Cornwall, which instigated my interest in the area. Now I always spend several weeks a year in Cornwall, usually around St Ives.

I was rarely happy at school until I went to art school. I was never a very confident child, and as my parents were publicans, we moved regularly to new areas. As soon as I got settled and made friends, it was time to move again. Each new school meant trying to catch up with their lessons and make new friends. It was a nightmare for me. Education was hardly a priority in my family and no one seemed to notice the difficulty I was having learning to read. With each new school I got further and further behind, until I eventually just gave up and spent most of my time in the art room. I left school at fifteen with just a school certificate in wood-work, art and geography.

How did you get into art school?

On leaving school in Newcastle-under-Lyme, I was advised to go to the Youth Employment Office to see if they could offer me anything that would use my artistic or carpentry skills. I was told to return in a week's time. The next day I rang the art school, and although I did not have the necessary qualifications, they eventually agreed to give me an interview.

To my delight, they accepted me on the strength of my sketchbooks. I discovered a week later that the job the Youth Employment Service had had in mind for me was cutting railway sleepers!

I thoroughly enjoyed the work at art school and concentrated first on silversmithing and then commercial design. Unfortunately, halfway through my art school course, yet again my parents were moving, this time to Duffield. At that time, there was no art school in Derby, so I was offered a place at Derby College of Art to continue my studies. I certainly would not have been accepted on my academic background.

What did these courses teach you?

I learned many things in both courses, but particularly useful at Newcastle-under-Lyme School of Art was the one day a week spent studying perspective; this has become invaluable in all my painting since.

At the course in Derby, we had one day and one evening per week of life drawing, which is also a vital part of an artist's training.

The other vital thing I learned was that the more time I spent painting, the more time I wanted to spend doing so.

When did you realise that it was possible to make a living from painting?

On leaving art college, I went to work at Bemrose in Derby as a print designer for three years. I had always painted and sold work in my spare time, mainly to customers of the Bridge Inn. During my time at Bemrose my paintings were selling well in several galleries and I soon began to see the possibilities. I decided that if I spent all my time painting, I could supply more galleries and, hopefully, soon equal my wage from Bemrose. I had no ties and at the age of twenty-one, against most people's advice, I became a full-time artist. Thirty-three years later, I still think that was one of my best decisions!

How did you decide what style of painting you would adopt?

In my early years as an artist, I painted a variety of subjects, but eventually settled on landscapes, as these interested me the most. The style was never a conscious decision; it just evolved over the years.

The first experience I had of living in an area with beautiful surroundings was at the Bridge Inn in Duffield, on the outskirts of the Peak District. It was wonderful living by the river and being able to experience nature's changing moods. This probably inspired me and helped me to want to spend all of my time painting. An artist never stops looking. It may have just snowed for an hour, but when the sun comes out and begins to melt the snow, everything starts to glisten on the trees, rooftops and rivers. In the evening, the sun sets, silhouetting the trees and church. On waking in the morning, the mist engulfing the whole scene creates a completely different world.

As soon as I had my own car at the age of twenty, I began to travel widely in the Peak District and discover its beauty and diversity.

Maybe if I had lived in a less beautiful area, I would have painted quite differently.

Have you always managed to make a living from painting?
Yes, although there were some very lean times in the early years. When I married Sue in 1974, and we bought our own house, we had to be very careful. My income was very unpredictable and as Sue was only nineteen, did not earn very much. She gave up work when Mark was born in 1976 and for seven years she remained at home looking after Mark and Michelle, born in 1978. We had some worrying times financially. Every time the telephone rang, we hoped that it was a gallery ringing to say they had sold a painting.

When the children were both at school, Sue returned to work and that certainly helped. It would have been impossible to hold on to paintings to stage one-man exhibitions without another source of income, so I used to have many smaller events with other artists and display small groups of paintings on a regular basis. Then I progressed to having two-man shows with Robin Gibbard, before I started having regular one-man exhibitions.

It has obviously been a lot easier as my exhibitions have become more successful, and the income from cards, calendars and prints has helped.

Are you influenced by market trends or personal taste?
I have painted professionally since 1969 and for 99 per cent of that time have managed to choose exactly what I wanted to paint. What sells well or what galleries want is never part of the consideration of what to paint. The reason I still get so much pleasure from my paintings is because I select everything, from the moody mountainous areas in Scotland to the flowers on the cliffs in Cornwall, and can go anywhere in between with no pressure from anyone as to what to paint. Artists very easily get channelled into painting a certain way, which is why there are so many who appear to be painting virtually the same subject over and over again. It is obviously not the easiest way to make a living, especially in the early days when struggling to support a young family, but it is very important to stay a free spirit and keep alive the enthusiasm which made you want to paint in the first place. The best way to do this is to be inspired by the landscape and not the sales. An artist friend of mine once took eight commissions at an exhibition preview, to reproduce virtually the same subject as a painting which had sold earlier in the evening. I could never understand how there could be any joy in painting the same thing over and over again. It turns into a boring and repetitive job when it can be so interesting and exciting. Surely an artist works better when he is left to paint what he wants. For this reason, I never accept commissions, although I am always eager to listen to suggestions of places that I might like to paint.

Which artists do you regard as your mentors?
I think I was very fortunate in the art teachers I had at Newcastle-under-Lyme School of Art. They seemed to have endless patience and were very encouraging, especially **Monty Grainger**, my personal tutor, who was a successful artist as well as a teacher. There was nothing I couldn't ask him. He always explained problems with drawings, and I still have endless sketches of the bone structures of birds, animals and people, and solutions to perspective problems. Monty took a few of us from art school on a two-week pot-holing trip to Gaping Gill in Yorkshire. This was my first introduction to the moors, which appeared incredibly wild, moody and atmospheric.

I sketched in the spare moments between pot-holing expeditions. We were told that the main pot, Gaping Gill, could fit St Paul's Cathedral inside. Shafts of light lit up the main river falling through the hole at the top of the cave. In our second week, we became guides and helped to make the measurements for future maps of the caves which were being produced at the time. We walked for miles, caught eels in the river and generally had a wonderful time. I feel sure that the bond I have with the moors must have started from that time spent camping halfway up Ingleborough mountain.

Later on, I would use Monty's house in Bradwell, North Derbyshire, as a base for sketching around the area. Sadly, Monty is not with us any more, but he definitely has had a lasting influence on my life.

Robin Gibbard had a huge influence on my early painting life. I first met him at the age of sixteen whilst living at the Bridge Inn in Duffield. He was painting by the river. We used to go painting and sketching together. It was Robin who introduced me to the Lake District, the Cotswolds, Wales and the Dent Valley, which helped to broaden my view of landscapes. For years, I almost felt like part of his family as I was always made to feel so welcome.

Some of our first exhibitions were in the side lounge at the Bridge Inn. The bar would close just after 11pm and we would set to work clearing the furniture and bringing in the display boards to transform it into a gallery, staying up into the small hours to hang the exhibition.

Robin and I helped to start the Derbyshire Group of Artists together, an organisation that enabled us to stage many varied exhibitions around the country. The group comprised eight enthusiastic artists, who shared the responsibility and expense of staging exhibitions. I enjoyed listening to their varied views on art and regularly encouraged them to criticise my work.

After several years with the Derbyshire Group, we left to stage many two-man exhibitions in various galleries. This continued for several years until into the early eighties when I began to have successful one-man shows.

For many years, I would ask Robin to criticise my paintings, to analyse them and identify faults.

In 1979, I went to an impressive exhibition by **Wilfred Ball** and invited him to come sketching with me one frosty, misty November day to Chee Dale. Wilf's enthusiasm and sheer excitement for the landscape was inspirational.

We must have walked thousands of miles together over the years. Wilf's enthusiasm could be seen and experienced every second he was in the countryside. The way he could describe a mountain would make you want to paint it before you had even seen it. He was a brilliant person with whom to experience the landscape, and always wanted to show me subjects. We had the advantage of two pairs of eyes seeking out material to paint and would discuss continuously what inspired us.

He made an excellent critic. I often took my paintings to his house, where Wilf and his wife Vicky would spend lunchtime discussing my paintings. Then I would go to his studio and return the favour. I feel sure that my work benefited greatly from Wilf's influence and consider myself fortunate to have known him – I miss him very much.

Do you regularly go painting and sketching with other artists?
I have always enjoyed going on trips with other artists. As already mentioned I used to go out sketching with Wilfred Ball and Robin Gibbard regularly, but over the years I have enjoyed painting with many artists, especially my brother Jim, Andrew Macara and his late brother Gordon, and in latter years my son Mark who is also an artist.

Did you influence your son in his choice of career?
Mark thought everyone's dad had a studio until he was about four! He always had a great interest in art from a very early age and could always see the possibilities of making a career as an artist by my example. After

studying illustration at university, he always had our encouragement to do whatever he wanted. He decided to try painting for a year to see if he could make a go of it. Mark has the same strong urge to paint that I had, and, as mentioned, the more you paint, the more you want to. We often go out painting together, and it's a joy to see him enjoying a considerable amount of success for a young artist.

Do you paint every day?

I usually paint in normal working hours five days a week, and try to keep the weekends free, although framing, varnishing and suchlike quite often get done in evenings and weekends. When painting out on location, however, my hours are determined by the travelling distance, light and weather conditions. My family and friends are quite used to me cancelling arrangements when I am still up on the moors at 9pm.

How do you decide what to paint?

On location, I just walk until something takes my eye and I start painting. I quite often don't know what I am looking for, but it usually involves colour, light and reflections. When painting in my studio, I look through my sketches, which always bring back vivid memories of what inspired me to sketch them in the first place.

When do you paint on location and when in your studio?

I try never to miss an opportunity to paint on location. I avoid as many appointments or interruptions as possible during spring, summer and early autumn and I am sure people regularly think I am being awkward, but you can guarantee if there is one sunny day in the week, it will be the one day when something else is arranged. Fortunately, my wife takes away most of the hassle, so that I can spend my time concentrating on painting. I prefer a mainly dry day to complete a painting outside, so during spring and summer I go off into the Peak District as much as possible, and regularly go on painting trips anywhere from Cornwall to Scotland to spend a couple of weeks on location.

Sketching is very useful to record fleeting light effects and atmospheres, which are gone before you could capture them on canvas. Often in showery weather it would be impossible to paint, but a sketch can show the changing skies and light effects. The most incredible effect might only last for a few minutes, but with my pencil and sketchbook, I can capture enough to be able to paint it later. Back in my studio, my sketch will remind me of what really inspired me and, together with my imagination and experiences, will give me all I need to complete a canvas.

Most of my larger paintings are done from sketches as they are too big to paint on location

How do you design a painting in the studio?

I always start with a sketch done on location, with photographs used only for occasional reference. Sometimes the sketch has enough information for me to start painting straight away. More usually, I do a design sketch, which determines the proportions and layout.

I always mark the centre point and divide the sketch into four to make it easier to transfer the subject onto the canvas. Sometimes two field sketches are combined, for example a sketch of some farm animals might be placed in a landscape and the position of these would be decided in the design sketch.

Once I have done a working sketch, I rarely stray from this original design during work on the painting. I usually draw out the design in paint very roughly on the canvas, marking the centre point very clearly. After that, I just start painting in whatever way I choose. Most commonly the sky would be done first, because it can influence all the colours in the rest of the painting. I rely greatly on my memory of the mood and atmosphere of a subject, which usually stays in my mind for a long time. But I often use my paintings done on location for colour reference in the studio later on.

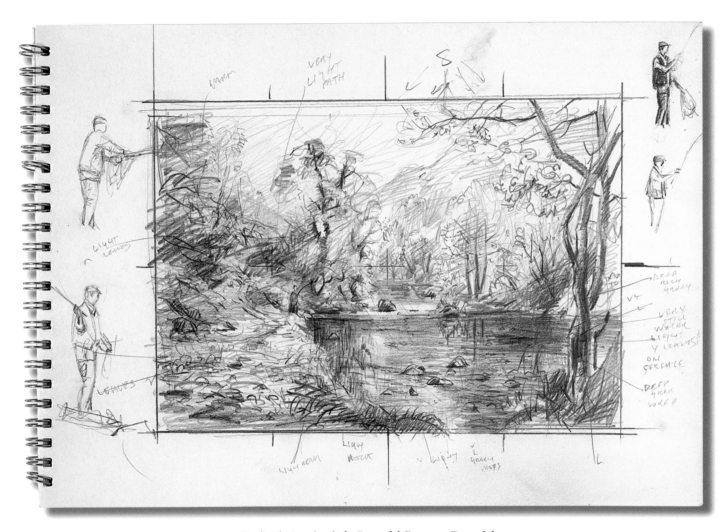

Studio design sketch for Peaceful Retreat, Dovedale

Why do you consider painting on location so important?

I have learned a huge amount about colour from painting on location. In my early years of painting, I tended to avoid painting brightly coloured flowers. Without plein-air painting, the colour of sunlit gorse in full bloom against a bright blue sky, a field of scarlet poppies or the beautiful rich colours of the heather, would be unattainable. The colours are hard to imagine without observing directly from life.

The sea, waterfalls or any fast-flowing water all require the artist to capture movement. It is very difficult to achieve from just a sketch, but seems to be no problem when painting from life.

Of course, all the experience of painting on location is an enormous help when painting from sketches in the studio. I often surround my easel with plein-air paintings to help with the colours in studio paintings.

Are you ever disappointed with a painting?

There have been plenty of difficult paintings over the years, but after a lifetime of experience you learn how to put most of them right. If I am not happy with a painting, I will usually show one of my artist friends and ask them to criticise as much as possible.

Many years ago, I ripped up a large watercolour that I had spent several days on. My daughter rescued it from the bin and turned it into a jigsaw puzzle with her friends.

Sometimes I have been really pleased with a painting and then when Sue returns from work, she will say that there is some part of it she is not keen on. Other times, when I think I have had a terrible day, she will really like what I have done. It is not always possible for me to tell immediately whether I have created a good painting or not as it is hard not to be influenced by how much I enjoyed doing it. Part of the fun in painting is that it is always a challenge.

One of the most frequently asked questions at an exhibition is 'How long did it take to paint that?' Anyone who paints knows that sometimes the most effective paintings, usually done on location, can be completed very quickly. When in front of a subject, I have to paint extremely quickly to capture the effect, but it is the experience that goes into the painting, not the length of time spent on that particular canvas which determines its effectiveness.

Do you have any special equipment for painting on location?

There is a tremendous amount of equipment needed for painting out on location. I have a list of forty-five items that I take when painting outside and I tick each one off before I go out. It is very frustrating to drive for an hour and then walk for another hour, only to find that some vital piece of equipment is missing. One day on a trip to paint water lilies in a lake, I walked a long way with my equipment, only to realise that I had forgotten my easel. I had to tie my canvas to a tree! Painting bluebells in a local wood, I was well into the picture before discovering I had forgotten the white paint. I just left everything where it was and went to an art shop to buy some – when I returned everything was just as I had left it.

All the equipment has to be as light as possible, as I often carry it for miles before deciding on a subject. In this country, you have to be prepared for all weathers, so I carry everything from suncream and insect repellant to waterproof coat and umbrella.

Over the years I have discovered various ways of making the job easier. The most important thing is to protect the finished painting, and I have a wooden canvas carrier to hold the painting as I walk back to the car. Once after a day's painting, a book in the boot of my car slid across my wet picture as I was driving home, and ruined it. After that I made a wooden case to fit in my car, which securely contains and protects any size of canvas.

Out on location at Baslow Edge

Are you very particular about your choice of materials?

I always use top-quality materials to ensure that my paintings will last. The canvasses I use are expensive but are robust and made of either fine or medium linen, depending on the subject.

My selection of oil colours has hardly changed since I first started painting. I always use Winsor & Newton artist-quality oils in cerulean and cobalt blue, French ultramarine, burnt sienna, cadmium red, alizarin crimson, Winsor yellow, yellow ochre and titanium white, with occasional use of a few others.

To apply the oil paint, I mainly use a palette knife. I prefer the ones that are worn thin by years of use, which makes them very flexible. My brushes are filberts, hogshair and sable.

Do you encounter any problems accessing private land?

Plenty. I was once given permission to paint on a farm, until the farmer realised that the subject I had in mind was a field of poppies. He then withdrew his permission, saying it highlighted an example of bad farming.

Once I was painting round bales on an estate farm, with permission from the farmer. Halfway through my painting, I saw this irate man coming towards me with two dogs and a horsewhip in his hand, accusing me of scaring the partridges even though they were pecking round my feet. Next he accused me of trespassing and marched me off the land with my incomplete painting. When I returned home, I managed, after a few telephone calls to get permission from the estate owner to override any gamekeeper on his land. I returned the next day and started painting, when who should come storming down the hill shouting, 'I thought I told you yesterday!' When I told him where my permission had come from, he then became very friendly and wanted to chat, but I took great delight in saying, 'Do you mind, you are disturbing me, I am very busy!'

In the late seventies, I was painting poppies in a rape field on a farm where I had permission to go anytime. About an hour into the painting, a helicopter started hovering overhead. Minutes later, the farm manager came running over to me looking very worried. He explained in a very stern voice that I must abandon everything and get out of the area immediately. The helicopter was spraying the crops and we had to run for about half a mile to get to a safe distance. I was not allowed back for twenty-four hours, when it was considered OK to return. It certainly made me wary of venturing onto farmland unannounced.

In Monsal Dale with Gordon Macara many years ago, we wanted to paint the view from the far bank. We didn't know who owned the land, but we ventured anyway. The position was brilliant, but halfway through the painting, a man with a large dog was threatening to throw us in the river, because we were on the wrong side of the water and were trespassing. Fortunately he allowed us to stay long enough to finish the paintings we had started. Sometimes it is virtually impossible to find out who owns the land, and the sunshine won't wait.

If I ever use a camera to record farm life, I am generally very careful what I photograph. I once had a farmer's wife cover herself with a coat and threaten to set the dogs on me. On several occasions I have had a shotgun pointed at me, accompanied by some swear-words. If I go into a similar situation with a sketchbook, there is no problem and people are always very friendly, offering to show me the their favourite spots.

Where do you exhibit your work?
Over the thirty-three years that I have been painting professionally, I have exhibited in many galleries around the country.

When I first started, I used to sell most of my work at the Halford House Gallery at Bourton-on-the-Water in the Cotswolds, and had many successful one-man exhibitions, which were virtual sellouts. My mother opened a shop in Duffield in 1972, originally as an antique shop, now a gallery, and I have taken part in many successful exhibitions there.

In 1982, I started to sell work in the Granby Gallery in Bakewell, Derbyshire, and had my first exhibition of watercolours there in 1986. It was a resounding success and I have had many successful exhibitions there since. I now have a biennial one-man exhibition at the Granby Gallery, which gives me the freedom to exhibit all of my work, and people who visit the exhibitions see a true representation of the previous two years' work. It is always a joy to sell the pictures that might not have been the obvious choices, but are my personal favourites.

I have encountered only two really exceptional gallery owners and Michael Mosley is definitely number one. It isn't just the gallery that is important, but the proprietor. In my experience, when an owner changes, everything changes. Michael goes to great lengths to ensure the success of exhibitions; all I have to do is paint and frame the pictures. I don't have to worry about any aspect of the exhibition as I know he will be on top of everything. Since I started exhibiting at Granby Gallery, my work has been extensively reproduced as fine art prints, cards and calendars without me having to get too involved. If anyone rings me about anything concerning exhibitions, prints or suchlike, I can just pass them on to Mike. We understand each other very well after all these years and both get an immense amount of pleasure from the exhibitions.

The Peak District & Pennines are obviously favourite areas of yours; which other places do you like to paint?
Although the Peak District is very familiar to me and will probably always be my favourite area, there are many other places that I love to capture on canvas.

Once I have found an interesting area, I tend to return many times and find that my interest in painting those places grows as they become more familiar.

Wherever I go, I generally tend to choose the wild, unspoilt spots for my subjects. The areas I visit vary from year to year, with the exception of Cornwall, which has always been a regular fixture.

I never fail to be impressed by Scotland and the Lake District, but in the last few years I have also developed an interest in the coastal marshland in Norfolk and Suffolk.

My sketchbook is almost always with me, and I am always keen to visit new areas which might spark my interest. We are very fortunate in Britain to have such a varied landscape in a relatively small area.

Painting on location on Zennor Head in Cornwall

The Harbour, Thornham, Norfolk   *12 x 24in   Oil*

Thornham is a favourite place of mine. It is very peaceful and unspoilt and I love
to paint the old boats and the reflections in the muddy creeks at low tide.

Southwold Harbour, Suffolk   *18 x 24in Oil*

When I first saw Southwold Harbour, I was fascinated by the old wooden landing stages reaching out across the banks of the River Blyth. Painting the reflections of the dramatic Suffolk sky in the water and mud presented an interesting challenge.

The Reedbeds of Westwood Marshes near Walberswick, Suffolk   *18 x 24in Oil*

The strength of this subject comes from the stark shape of the ruined mill against the sunlight.
Sketching is by far the best way for me to capture a scene like this. The light effects last only for a short time,
so I use a combination of a sketch and my memory to paint the picture in the studio.

Scafell Pike from Eskdale, the Lake District *16 x 20in Oil*

The rugged Lake District scenery offers a wealth of dramatic subjects, Eskdale being a typical example.

The Picnic, Buttermere, the Lake District *20 x 30in Oil*

Wilfred Ball showed me this beautiful spot. It was one of his favourite places, so I included him in this painting.

Highland Cattle, Glencoe, Scotland *24 x 30in Oil*

Driving through Glencoe, I glanced to one side and noticed the mist clinging to a distinctive looking mountain. As I walked along the track, I came across a herd of highland cattle. They stood there so proudly, almost blocking the path and helping to create a powerful Scottish scene.

Loch Carron, Plockton, Scotland   *10 x 12in   Oil*

Whenever visiting Scotland, I find Plockton hard to resist. Tucked away on
the West Coast on an inlet of Loch Carron, it has a unique atmosphere.

Sunflowers, The Vendée, France   *12 x 10in   Oil*

Travelling down to St Hilaire-de-Riez on our first family holiday in France, we passed
fields of brilliant yellow.   It soon became apparent that there were sunflowers everywhere
and I could hardly wait to start sketching.

Evening Light, St Hilaire-de-Riez, France   *12 x 16in Oil*

Our holidays spent camping in the Vendée were very relaxing. Lazy sunny days were spent having barbecues, swimming in the pool and taking Mark fishing in the lake, mornings and evenings. One evening the light was so good, that I left him fishing and wandered off to do some sketching. It was wonderful watching the shadows grow longer and the last of the sunlight warm the colours of everything it touched.

Clifftop Gorse near Rosemergy, Cornwall   *14 x 12in Oil*   **Porthmeor Beach, St Ives, Cornwall**   *20 x 18in Oil*

These were painted on location on one of my many trips to Cornwall with Mark.

We usually stay in either St Ives or Zennor and never fail to be impressed by the vivid colours of the sea, sky and clifftop flowers.

Longships Lighthouse, near Land's End, Cornwall   *12 x 10in   Oil*   **Low Tide, Porthtowan, Cornwall**   *14 x 10in   Oil*

I like finding subjects high on the cliffs, as it allows me an uninterrupted view and provides a good vantage point from which to see the changing skies. Painting Longships Lighthouse, I set up on the steep slopes of the cliffs above the rock called the Irish Lady. It gave me a brilliant view, but any brushes or paints that I dropped were never to be seen again!

Andrew Macara's View

When we look at a painting by Rex Preston our spirits are lifted. It is not just his selection of the subject matter that causes this but in his combination of brushstrokes with just the right amount of paint. It is in the textureand love of the paint and the way it is applied. I am referring to the oil paintings here, but Rex is also a master in the use of watercolour and acrylic. One outstanding skill he has is in the depiction of water. Whether the water is still or running or cascading down a waterfall, it appears wet! When sunlight falls on the water, we see either the reflection from the surface or the light passing through the water to the river bed. We see the shadows on the river bed and all that is of visual interest. These paintings are not intended to shock as conceptual works do. They convey the artist's visual excitement with the world. The skill required to do this does not come easily. This is the fruit of many years of observation, of working outdoors in all weathers, painting in front of the subject.

Andrew Macara RBA NEAC

Reflections of Autumn, New Forest, Hampshire *18 x 36in Oil*

Robin Gibbard meets Rex Preston

On a perfect summer's day, I decided to paint the Bridge Inn at Duffield from the other side of the River Derwent, looking north. At the time, in the 1960s, I was a member of the Derby Sketching Club and sketched and painted in watercolours the local landscape and anywhere on holidays that appealed to me.

After a while a lanky youth with dark curly hair came strolling along to look over my shoulder and made some comment, which developed into a conversation. The youth invited me to view his own collection of oils at the Inn. Expecting to see an exhibition, it was with surprise that I was taken to a large room, which served primarily as studio and storage, but also as a bedroom.

Rex, as it turned out to be, was obviously a devoted artist, bursting with latent talent and enthusiasm, but needing some directional guidance. An introduction to Derby Sketching Club sufficed for a short while, until it merged with another club and the sketching meetings became rather crowded. We both left the club and formed a small nucleus of artists called the Derbyshire Group of Artists. During the interim period, Rex invited me to share an exhibition at his home, the Bridge Inn, by way of an experiment. It meant waiting until the last customer had left, then at about midnight moving chairs, stools and tables up to the landing, bringing down display boards and screwing them together in one of the public rooms. At about 2 or 3am the paintings were introduced and the arguments started as to where to hang them. Pictures were rearranged several times until an agreed satisfactory arrangement was reached. By 8am the pricing and labelling had been done and we got our own breakfast, this being the order of the day, as each member of the household had their allocated jobs to do. The exhibition was a success, quite a few paintings being sold to local visitors.

Rex invested his money in a second-hand caravan, which he pitched by the river bank, then promptly tore out all the internal walls to make a first-class studio.

It was in this environment that he painted his first one-man show staged at Bourton-on-the-Water in the Cotswolds. I had dealt with Halford House Gallery for a number of years and felt Rex was ready to join me there. A blinding success set Rex on the road to a professional career that has developed into the status that he only dreamed about in the early days in his late teens.

My memories of those days are hazy now, but some still linger: sketching at Derby County Show outside a marquee, surrounded by a quagmire of mud; beating Rex at pool in the Sun Inn in Dent after Rex had just taught me to play and after three pints of Old Peculiar each! There was the occasion when a booked exhibition in Cheshire was cancelled at the last minute and nearly a hundred paintings had to be disposed of. A phone call to a Nottingham gallery resulted in an instant change of venue and more driving. It solved the acute problem, but not the financial one as few paintings were sold owing to the lack of advertising. Then there was the embarrassing situation following a TV interview and a day's filming of painting on location, which we hoped would promote our forthcoming exhibition in Coventry. Both of us were worth several thousand pounds in pictures, but were stony broke and couldn't even buy a round of drinks for the film crew.

The years spent mounting exhibitions with the Derbyshire Group of Artists undoubtedly taught Rex the ropes in transporting, framing and hanging exhibitions and stood him in good stead when he finally emerged as a confident and successful artist. His paintings will live forever.

Robin Gibbard

The Peak District and Southern Pennines

Mountain Ash, Curbar Edge, Derbyshire   *14 x 12in Oil*

Before moving to Derbyshire with my family at the age of fifteen, I knew very little about the Peak District. Living in this area opened my eyes to the beauty of the landscape. Previously my sketchbooks had been filled with buildings, people and interiors, but I soon realised what a beautiful and immensely varied landscape the Peak District had to offer.

Although I enjoy painting many other areas, nowhere quite offers the diversity of the Peak District, from the wild open spaces of the bleak moorland to the more well-known dales, from the limestone villages to the gritstone edges.

I particularly enjoy the wild, unspoilt and less accessible places, which require a long walk to reach, but are well worth the effort.

For me the Peak District is fascinating in all seasons and in all weathers.

Peaceful Retreat, Dovedale, Derbyshire   *20 x 30in Oil*

Rape Field, Belper Lane End, Derbyshire (left)   *14 x 12in Oil*

It is a real challenge to attempt to paint the brilliance of colour in an oilseed rape field.   The dark shapes of the trees and hedgerows provide contrast against the dazzling yellow. It took quite a while to search for the best spot from which to paint these five rape fields.

When trying to mix the strength of yellow, the paint never seems to be bright enough. It always appears dull when compared to the intensity of colour in the flowers in front of me. Yet when I take the painting back to the studio, the colours seem incredibly vibrant.

Field of Poppies, Derbyshire (near right)   *20 x 18in Oil*
Summer Haze, Belper Lane End, Derbyshire (far right)
20 x 18in Oil

I had not initially realised that, having painted these two canvasses out on location on different days, they fitted together exactly. They were exhibited together and had extra impact as a pair.

These fields are near the top of a hill and I love the wonderful feeling of open space around me whenever I go there.

I could have spent weeks studying the variety of reds. My normal palette would include cadmium red and alizarin crimson mixed with Winsor yellow, but found that I was trying Winsor yellow deep and Winsor orange to achieve the strength of colour of the sunlight on the flowers.

A Sharp Frost, Derbyshire   *16 x 24in   Oil*

Opening the curtains one December morning, revealed that everything was covered with a thick frost, and the dawn sky looked wonderful. After a quick breakfast, I put on as many layers of clothing as possible and set off with my sketchbook to the local park. It was even colder than it looked, and as the sun rose, I saw a variety of potential subjects.

Standing on a stone bridge which crossed the brook, I saw a line of Canada geese perched on top of a waterfall, with a further large group in the calm water above. I walked around carefully to get a better view without disturbing them. They looked so content, going about their daily routine of cleaning and preening, bathed in the early morning sunlight.

The waterfall sparkled as it fell and the light from the sunrise caught almost every tree in my view, filling the frosty park with a warm glow. With all the golden light around me, I almost forgot just how cold it was, but my hands and feet kept reminding me. The sketch had to be completed quickly before the frost started to melt and the light began to change.

Whilst I was sketching, a bank vole appeared and sat near me, happily feeding. I moved to sharpen my pencil and it shot down a hole.

A man taking his dog for a morning walk made his way across the bridge and I wondered whether he was appreciating the beautiful winter colours or was just lost in his thoughts.

Farmland near Shottle, Derbyshire *12 x 16in Oil*

Springtime, Rakestones Farm near Kirk Ireton, Derbyshire   *14 x 16in Oil*

Autumn Walk, Cromford Canal, Derbyshire   *24 x 36in Oil*

On this particular day, I had thought that it was maybe too late in the year to be sketching autumn colours. However, as I walked along Cromford Canal past mainly bare trees, I stopped to admire a large oak in full autumn hue reflecting in the still water of the canal. With the soft November light coming through the mist, I was immediately inspired to set to work on this subject.

Cromford has a main road, a minor road, a river, a footpath and a railway line all running parallel to the canal. Whilst I was engrossed sketching this scene, there came an enormous roar, seemingly from nowhere. I realised I was standing on a viaduct: the main railway line goes through a tunnel and came out right underneath where I was standing.

Lathkill Dale, Derbyshire *20 x 30in Oil*

Thorpe Cloud, Derbyshire   *20 x 30in Oil*

I have usually resisted painting the stepping stones in Dovedale as they make such an obvious subject.
Early on this November morning, however, the sight of Thorpe Cloud in the mist was very impressive.

Hints of Autumn, Dovedale, Derbyshire *20 x 30in Oil*

Dovedale is probably the most accessible and popular valley in Derbyshire, with crowds of people treading its path. For most of the time it could hardly be described as tranquil or peaceful, but in the early morning, before people descend from every direction, it does display the quiet atmosphere shown in this picture.

I walked along the dale for about a mile beyond the famous stepping stones. The place I chose to sketch was just past a bend in the river, where it was so still that there was hardly a ripple in the water.

When I had been quietly drawing for a while, two early-morning walkers appeared, who I am sure had no idea that they were being sketched for inclusion in my painting.

The water was so still that it gave an almost perfect reflection, interrupted only by a few leaves gently floating on the surface.

On completing my sketch, I was keen to get back to my studio to make a start on a large canvas for this idyllic subject.

Grazing in the Sunshine, Dovedale, Derbyshire   *8 x 10in Oil*

October Sunshine, Monsal Dale, Derbyshire   *18 x 24in Oil*

Sunshine on a Frosty Day, Dovedale, Derbyshire   *12 x 16in Oil*

I never paint winter scenes on location, as it is far too cold to sit still in one position all day and the light effects usually last for such a short time. A sketch with colour-notes and my memory are usually all I need to complete a painting.

Early Spring, Wolfscote Dale, Derbyshire   *14 x 16in Oil*

Cottages in Alport, Derbyshire   *10 x 12in Oil*

I have painted Alport village many times, in all seasons. This blossom tree by the river is perfectly situated amongst the old stone buildings and makes an interesting subject in spring, from almost every angle.

Blossom at Alport, Derbyshire   *20 x 18in   Oil*

Painting Cottages at Alport

Cottages at Alport, Derbyshire   *10 x 12in   Oil*

One June morning when I had intended to complete a series of poppy paintings, I was in for a big disappointment. The farmer had mowed the field and the vibrant colour had disappeared. I wanted to paint something colourful and immediately thought of Alport, where the cottages were always covered in flowers in the summer.

I soon had my easel set up on the side of the road near a bend. It was not the safest place to choose, so I put a red warning triangle on the road to ensure that I could safely finish my painting.

Several of the villagers chatted to me as they passed by and showed great interest in my work in progress.

My first painting in Bradford Dale

Marsh Marigolds *10 x 14in Oil*

The first time I ever went to Bradford Dale was with my wife, Sue. It was a sunny day towards the end of March and probably the first time we had actually gone out walking without either of the children, who were both busy doing other things.

As we walked up the dale, there appeared to be endless subjects and it seemed incredible that I had never been here before after almost thirty years of painting Derbyshire. As we sat in the café having a cup of tea, I was already planning when I could come back with my paints.

Returning soon afterwards, I found an area of marsh marigolds that looked particularly interesting. At first I could not find the right subject, but a week or so later I went with my brother Jim and we walked up and down the dale on both sides of the river. The marigolds were fully open and the colour was amazing. Over the next few weeks, we went back several times and a stretch of river bank became our studio. There seemed to be a fresh subject every time we looked. Eventually we both dispensed with the usual land-scape format of sky, middle distance and foreground and concentrated solely on the flowers (see opposite and overleaf). The reflections of the blue sky in the water shown in all the paintings was all that was required to illustrate the clear spring day, with the sunlight creating interesting light-and-shade effects through the wooded bank.

I have been back to Bradford Dale many times since and always been pleased with the subjects I have found.

Marsh Marigolds in Bradford Dale   *16 x 20in Oil*

Spring in Bradford Dale, Derbyshire *10 x 8in Oil*

Shades of Autumn, Bradford Dale   *18 x 36in Oil*

The sun was just beginning to break through the thick mist as I parked the car in Alport village one autumn morning. Having decided to walk up Bradford Dale, I set off towards Youlgreave, going over the large stone slabs of the clapper bridge and continuing up the dale. Glancing back I noticed the River Bradford reflecting the warm misty sky, with the trees in the distance still partially hidden in the mist. I was just about to begin sketching, when I noticed that high above the dale, the sunlight was just catching the cottages and the surrounding trees. I climbed up the side of the dale to get a better view and sat on a tree stump to sketch, using two pages to take in the full expanse of the scene.

It was interesting to observe the people passing through the dale. Some walked past deep in conversation, seemingly oblivious to the surrounding beauty, others noticed me sitting above them and remarked how special the dale looked on that particular morning.

At times like this I realise that, however beautiful the location, the subject comes from the changing light and atmosphere, which make each new day unique.

After sitting for an hour or so, I was getting very cold and as soon as my sketch was finished, I rushed to the café up the hill for a hot cup of tea.

Frosty Morning, Bradford Dale, Derbyshire   *14 x 24in Oil*

Early Morning, Bradford Dale, Derbyshire *16 x 20in Oil*

Water's Edge, Bradford Dale, Derbyshire   *10 x 12in Oil*

Autumn, Middleton-by-Youlgreave, Derbyshire   *18 x 24in Oil*

Middleton-by-Youlgreave, Derbyshire *14 x 24in Oil*

I meet all kinds of interesting people when I am out sketching, a pleasant change from being alone in my studio.

One autumn day I was leaning on my car, sketching the buildings and trees around the square in Middleton-by-Youlgreave, when a local man came across for a chat. He told me some village history, including the fact that the building on the right of my subject used to be the Bateman's Arms and was last used as an inn over a hundred years ago.

I was sketching a village dog and explained to the man that I liked to put local people and animals in my paintings. He immediately asked where he should stand. I suggested that the bus stop might be a good spot and he was soon in position. When I signalled to him that I had finished my sketch, he wandered off down the lane.

A week or two later, Sue and I were visiting an exhibition in Bakewell on a very wet day. I suggested that we take a detour on the way back to see how the square in Middleton would look after the rain. It looked even better than I had hoped. Unfortunately, as we were in Sue's car, I had no sketch-book with me. Improvisation was required and so I used the inside of a tissue box and a ballpoint pen to record the wet road. This information helped me to finish my painting. Sometimes several sketches and visits are necessary to achieve the desired effect.

Spring, Bakewell, Derbyshire *14 x 10in Oil*

One spring morning, I decided to drive to Bakewell to paint Haddon House orchard, where the pear blossom was in full bloom. I arrived around 8.30am and the clear blue sky looked set to last for the day. There was a haze on the surrounding hills and it appeared a promising start to a day's painting.

Finding a suitable spot, however, proved more difficult. I spent quite a long time moving from one place to another, unable to settle. I was trying to find a position from which the blossom could be seen against the hazy background and where I could include some of the bluebells in the foreground. Having explored a wood to the far side of the orchard and spent some time clearing the dead branches to allow a view through the trees, I was still not satisfied and moved to the top of the wood, which at last gave me the subject I wanted.

I set up my easel in an area of bluebells, near a small stream. A single pear tree against the hazy blues and greys of the distance was originally my focal point until a newborn lamb with its mother appeared.

In the middle distance, the trunks of the damson trees created a dark pattern against the sunlit blossom of a huge old pear tree at the bottom of the orchard.

Snowscene, Ashford-in-the-Water, Derbyshire   *18 x 24in Oil*

Evening Reflections, River Wye, Bakewell, Derbyshire *20 x 24in Oil*

Autumn in Winster, Derbyshire   *14 x 30in   Oil*

Walking along the Limestone Way from Youlgreave to Winster, I stopped to sketch this farm scene. Although I had driven through Winster on numerous occasions, as usual, it was not until I put my boots on that I found the best subject. The limestone walls that are such a feature of the Peak District add a special character to the farmland.

This sketch was done from the shelter of my car. A good way to record wet weather without getting soaked.

Sunshine After the Rain, Sheldon, Derbyshire *18 x 24in Oil*

Chatsworth Stream, Derbyshire (left)   *12 x 10in Oil*
Spring Flowers, Chatsworth, Derbyshire (right)   *12 x 16in Oil*

Having gained permission from the Duke of Devonshire to paint at Chatsworth, I always check in at the Forestry Office first, to let them know that I am around and to ensure that I do not get mistaken for a poacher.

The stream running through the woods has provided me with endless subjects, particularly in early spring when there is a profusion of bluebells. The wood is transformed into a blaze of colour by the spring sunshine.

When painting the sunlight through the trees, it is important to work quickly as the light is constantly changing. I use a large brush to cover the canvas quickly, showing roughly the effect I want, I can then take more time to record the detail. To achieve the blue, I mix ultramarine with alizarin crimson. The dappled light catching the carpet of spring flowers on the ground and the gently flowing stream made an excellent subject.

Autumn at Chatsworth   *18 x 36in   Oil*

I was amazed by the variety of autumn colour in
front of me whilst sketching at Chatsworth.

The River Wye rushes along its rocky river bed through Chee Dale, between the high limestone cliffs which open up into deep gorges.
Parts of this wild dale are inaccessible when the water is high, as the stepping stones alongside the cliffs become submerged.

Shades of Autumn, River Wye, Chee Dale, Derbyshire *12 x 16in Oil*

Home for Lunch, Benty Grange Farm, Monyash, Derbyshire   *18 x 24in Oil*

Sunny Afternoon, Parkhouse Hill, Derbyshire   *12 x 16in   Oil*

Morning Mist, Curbar Edge, Derbyshire   *12 x 10in   Oil*

Walk Along Stanage Edge, Derbyshire   *16 x 24in   Oil*

I had waited a long time to see Curbar Edge in the mist; those days that start off with
a thick mist and then clear completely as the sun breaks through are amazing.
The sky reflects beautifully in these still moorland pools.

I was exploring the area around Curbar and Froggatt Edges, when I discovered this tall silver
birch standing out of the woods below the edge. Against the gentle soft-toned background,
it shone like a beacon, its colour emphasised by the late-afternoon sun.

Autumn Colours, Froggatt Edge   *16 x 20in Oil*

Cotton Grass, White Edge Moor, Derbyshire   *16 x 20in Oil*

Changing Light, Curbar Edge, Derbyshire   *14 x 16in Oil*

Ramblers on Derwent Moor, Derbyshire   *18 x 24in Oil*

I had been walking for several hours in the snow on Derwent Moor, when the clouds suddenly parted, with the most dramatic effect. Rays of sunlight shone through, illuminating Crook Hill, which stood out against the pastel blue-grey of Win Hill in the shade.

The distant colour of Derwent Edge was a deep grey in the shadow of the clouds. The brilliant sunshine on the foreground emphasised the burnt siennas and deep umbers of the moorland heather, which contrasted with the glare of the snow. The warm winter sun reflected in the frozen pool, adding to this amazing atmosphere.

A line of ramblers in random groups filed across my view, the edge of each figure being caught by the brilliance of the sun.

The End of the Day, White Edge Moor, Derbyshire   *24 x 30in Oil*

Reflected Glow, Derwent Moors, Derbyshire *16 x 30in Oil*

Driving along a moorland road, I saw a windswept silver birch standing alone on the moor. Having noticed it several times before, I decided to investigate whether it could be used successfully in a painting. It was all twisted and gnarled and well worth a sketch on its own. The silver trunk stood out against the dark moorland and the tree seemed to tell a story of the wild winds and extremes of weather. Close by were several peat-coloured pools, which I thought I could also use, but by now the light had faded and I decided to return another day.

Next time I went with Wilf, my brother Jim and son Mark and soon we were all working. I sketched the two pools
reflecting the colours of the sky, which made the nearest pool look a deep indigo and the other a rich blue.
Combined with the varied strong colours of the moor, it looked very promising. Mark was producing a dramatic dark
study, capturing well the mood of the area. My second sketch of the day was of the silver birch.
I intended to join the two together for one large canvas (see painting overleaf).

Moorland Pools, Derbyshire   *12 x 30in   Oil*

View from the Moors, Stanage Edge, Derbyshire   *18 x 36in Oil*

When walking along these edges, I always get the feeling of being on top of the world.

These two paintings show the panoramic views from Stanage Edge, which are especially stunning in the evening light.

Moorland Sunset, Derbyshire *20 x 30in Oil*

This wonderful sunset was spoilt only by the invasion of midges whilst I was sketching, which can be a real problem on summer evenings.

Wet Summer's Day, Curbar Edge, Derbyshire   *14 x 12in Oil*

I almost abandoned this painting when it started to rain, but the shades of purple against
the misty grey sky persuaded me to continue. I had to hold an umbrella over my
easel for some of the time but, fortunately, most of the rain stayed in the distance.

Kinder Edge from Ashop Clough, Derbyshire   *18 x 20in Oil*

On this very windy day, the clouds were racing across the sky, creating shadows on the moorland,
and the sunlit grasses on the hillside made a brilliant contrast against the dark Kinder edges.

HIGHFIELD FARM, EDALE   SNOW

One winter day as I parked in Mam Tor car park, light snow was just starting to fall. I took the path up onto the moors in the opposite direction to Mam Tor. It had snowed several times over the past few days and I had to tread carefully. After about thirty minutes, I found myself in a blizzard and decided to abandon this unfamiliar path to find a route down into the valley of Edale. I felt safer in the lower parts of the moor, closer to civilisation.

I walked above two hillside farms, as it continued to snow heavily, but as I sheltered by a stone wall to eat my lunch, the snowfall began to ease, revealing an old stone barn full of character, with a farm further down the valley. As I lingered by this barn, hoping for a better light, I noticed a farmer staring up at me. He asked if I had lost the path, so I went down to explain what I was doing. He soon became very interested and suggested I pop down to his farmhouse later, where he showed me a calendar containing an illustration of his farm.

Meanwhile the sun was coming out, so the farmer went off to feed his animals, and I went back to try to find a position from which to clearly see the barn and the farm. I immediately noticed the large clouds, which seemed to dominate the whole valley. The sky changed from brightly lit clouds on the right to a bright blue sky on the left, with a huge cloud with a dark base in the centre. Lose Hill appeared in the distance, almost floodlit against the dark cloud. I stood for quite some time watching as the sun found different ways to shine through the heavy clouds behind me.

My only problem was the large plain area of snow in the foreground, so in my painting I decided to move a gate and muddy track from about a hundred yards away. It had deep puddles reflecting the sky and the deep ruts made by the farm machinery gave a perfect lead into this wild Derbyshire scene.

It is quite often difficult to tell who owns the land I walk on when looking for subjects. Where it is possible, I ask for permission to wander on the land, but often get questioned by farmers wondering what I am doing. Usually, as in this case, they are very helpful and make me very welcome.

Tending the Sheep, Highfield Farm, Edale, Derbyshire   *16 x 30in Oil*

Snowscene, Edale, Derbyshire   *12 x 24in Oil*

The height of the hills around Edale means that I can often find snow there when there is none to be seen elsewhere.

Cross-Country Skiing, Edale, Derbyshire *14 x 24in Oil*

The snowstorm that had engulfed me only minutes before had now moved towards Mam Tor and the vale of Edale on the right was bathed in sunshine. I was not expecting to see any skiers, but they made a welcome addition to my painting.

Cascading Icicles, Grindsbrook Clough, Edale *15 x 22in Watercolour*

When the streams around Kinder freeze, there are some magical effects. The character of this familiar place was completely transformed by the ice.

Snowscene, Chatsworth Park, Derbyshire   *15 x 22in Watercolour*

En route to Kinder, we only got as far as Chatsworth, when the thick snow prevented us from travelling any further.
It was a day of sunshine and snow showers and Chatsworth had been enchantingly transformed by the wintry weather.
I was fascinated by the way the warm, creamy light illuminated the snow.

Evening Light, Kinder, Derbyshire   *20 x 30in Oil*

Seal Moor, below Kinder, is a special favourite of mine, with the rugged edge towering above and excellent views of Fairbrook Naze.

I had been advised not to stay on the moors in the evening, but I know the paths down from this spot very well and experiencing the last light can be very rewarding.

I was sketching this scene when a farmer and his dog came slowly across the moor, checking on his sheep. The man sat on a rock and appeared totally content, in full control of his wild land and taking time to enjoy the mood of the moor where he spent his working day. He was obviously completely at home in this lonely environment. In contrast, his dog seemed eager to get home.

I was attracted to the pastel blues of the dramatic Kinder escarpment in the background. Seal Edge was on the left and Fairbrook Naze dominated the right. The mist was developing and blending the blues of the hills with the oranges and yellows of the sky. The warm glow across the foreground caught the moorland grasses, the bilberry and heather. As the area is very boggy, it was easy to find a pool to reflect the colours of the sky.

Nowhere could be more peaceful and gratifying than the moors on a summer evening.

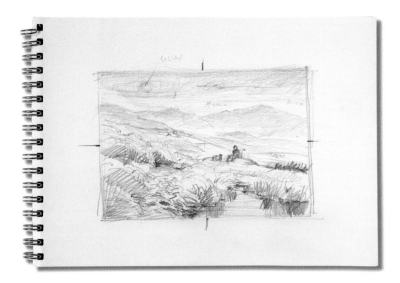

Clear Water, Fairbrook (left)   *15 x 11in Watercolour*
Evening in Fairbrook, Derbyshire (right)   *12 x 16in Oil*

This is one of the most beautiful valleys I have ever seen; it is very well hidden and accessed through a pine forest and over a footbridge. It is only a few miles long, but in August and September when the heather is in full bloom, it is absolutely stunning. The cascading water glistens as it finds its way over the rocks into the many deep, clear pools. The banks are lined with silver birch and mountain ash trees, and the distinctive shapes of the Kinder edges can be seen in the distance.

When Mark and Michelle were very young, in the eighties, this was one of our favourite picnic spots. We used to walk to a little sandy area by the side of a pool, which the children used to call the beach. They used to play happily for hours in the sunshine, damming up parts of the brook and playing in the water. It was always crystal clear and very cold, being mainly fed by springs. They would lift the rocks and watch small fish dart from underneath. It was always quiet and even on a bank holiday we would see very few people. Whenever I paint or sketch in Fairbrook now, fond memories of these times come flooding back.

Around 1996, Mark joined me to paint some of his first landscapes in Fairbrook.

Sunny Day, Fairbrook Valley, Derbyshire   *16 x 14in Oil*

August Morning, Derbyshire   *12 x 14in Oil*

I enjoy painting the clear water in Fairbrook, which would be very difficult from a sketch. Fortunately, in August and September, when the heather is out, there is usually enough fine weather to allow me to paint several times on location there.

Almond Blossom, Staffordshire   *14 x 24in Oil*

My daughter, Michelle, had an occasional day's holiday from school one day in April. Sue, my wife, was at work and my son, at a different school, was not on holiday. I suggested that the two of us went on a bicycle ride.

I drove to Waterhouses, where we hired our cycles, then rode down a narrow lane to a small village called Waterfall. This in turn led downhill to a ford, beside which nestled a small group of limestone cottages and farm buildings, called 'Back o' the Brook'.

We stopped by a bridge to eat our packed lunch and watched the newly-born lambs getting familiar with their new world.

The meadows were yellow with celandines. Most of the trees were still bare and their branches stood out on this hazy spring day. The soft pink blossom of the almond tree against the limestone cottage completed the scene. Just as well I had my sketchbook in my haversack, although I rarely go out without it.

An excellent subject would have been missed had we not stopped for lunch.

Highlander near Throwley Hall, Staffordshire   *12 x 10in Oil*

Driving along the stone-walled country lanes near Throwley Hall above the Manifold Valley,
I saw this stranger to the Staffordshire landscape, just standing there waiting to be sketched.

Ramshaw Rocks, Staffordshire   *12 x 16in Oil*

Ramshaw Rocks dominate the skyline high above Leek. I had to carry all my painting equipment up to almost the highest point to paint this picture, positioning myself behind a rock to shelter myself and my easel from the strong wind.

We spent a winter's day on the borders of Yorkshire and Derbyshire just driving around the country lanes trying not to waste what had turned out to be a cold and rainy day. We followed a lane that petered out at this farm, which we sketched through the car window. The building was full of character and I knew that I would have to return in better weather.

When I find an interesting area, I usually return again and again in different seasons and weathers. I have sketched the area around Bolsterstone many times. The buildings are in really interesting positions, built to withstand the wild moorland weather.

Summer Landscape near Bolsterstone, South Yorkshire   *18 x 36in   Oil*

This was a summer's day of sunshine and showers. I was surrounded by the rich colours of the bilberries,
gorse and heather of Whitwell Moor, in contrast to the blue shades of the distance.

The Northern Pennines

Bridge over the River Skirfare, Littondale, Yorkshire   *20 x 16in   Oil*

My first introduction to the Pennines was at the age of sixteen on a pot-holing trip to Gaping Gill with some art school friends. Camping halfway up Ingleborough mountain, I first experienced the Yorkshire fells and filled a sketchbook in a week. I have since made many trips to Yorkshire and Cumbria.

I am often inspired to paint the buildings in this area, as they are usually situated in such a way as to seem to belong to the landscape. I love their simple shapes, built to withstand the wind and rain.

The Howgills in Cumbria is a large group of hills with soft curves and smooth shapes, with a distinct character all of their own.

The Yorkshire Dales are full of stone walls, barns, farms and cottages and with their crystal-clear streams and rivers, I never need to search too long for a subject.

Howgills from Combe Scar, Cumbria *12 x 16in Oil*

Lambs at Littondale, Yorkshire   *11 x 7in Watercolour*

Early Morning, Littondale, Yorkshire *11 x 7in Watercolour*

The Packhorse Bridge, Yockenthwaite, Langstrothdale, Yorkshire

18 x 36in Oil

Yockenthwaite in Langstrothdale is a remote, unspoilt place. I imagine that maybe an artist could have painted this hundreds of years ago and it would not have looked very different.

On this particular day, the light was continually changing. The blue sky with sunlit clouds changed dramatically as a dark cloud loomed, casting a shadow over the far hillside, whilst the buildings and surrounding fells remained in full sunshine.

A farmer taking his sheep across the bridge to pastures new added life to the landscape.

Spring Flowers, Kilnsey Crag, Wharfedale, Yorkshire *12 x 14in Oil*

Waterfalls, Langstrothdale, North Yorkshire   *18 x 24in Oil*

Evening in the Dales, North Yorkshire   *18 x 36in Oil*

Ingleborough Peak from Black Shiver Moss, North Yorkshire   *16 x 20in Oil*

In Need of Repair, Angram, North Yorkshire   *10 x 14in Oil*

When walking in Yorkshire, I discovered a small group of stone cottages nestling below the moorland slopes close to the head of Swaledale. After having a good look round, I made my way up a track which led to the moors.

The colour of the sky was changing to a warm yellow as evening drew near. I passed a beautiful old stone farm built to withstand the wild moorland weather. By the farm, leaning against the stone wall at the edge of the track, were old tyres, wheels, fence posts and other discarded items. An ancient tractor had been left to rest at the side of the track.

After walking past, I turned to look at the farm, which now appeared as a strong, dark shape against the misty valley. The scene was filled with yellow light, which seemed to bring the worn-out tractor to life.

My first thought had been to paint the farm, but this old workhorse had so much character, I felt compelled to make it the main feature of my painting.

Dusk, Angram, North Yorkshire   *10 x 12in Oil*

Butterpots Farm, Deepdale, Cumbria   *20 x 36in Oil*

There is only one hen on this farm, named Henrietta. She has the complete run of the house and is regularly to be found sitting on the armchair. Miley, the farmer, had a steaming hot cup of tea waiting for me for when I had finished this sketch, as I was freezing.

Mucky Duck Farm, Cumbria (right)   *16 x 36in Oil*

On the way up to the Lake District, fellow artist Robin Gibbard had some paintings to deliver to the Fountain Gallery in Dent. Richard and Janet Thorpe, the owners of the gallery, offered to show us the area, which was completely new to me.

They took us along a narrow, gated Roman road which ran close to the River Dee and it soon became obvious to me that this would not be my last visit to Dentdale.

Knowing how much I liked to paint water, Richard wanted to take me to a nearby farm. He explained en route that they always referred to it as 'Mucky Duck Farm', although the farmer might not approve.

We drove down a tree-lined lane, which left the foreground in the shade. The sun managed to shine through the trees, illuminating the moss-covered stone wall and the rich colour of the fallen leaves. A meadow sloped towards a delightful pond lined with reeds, where geese and ducks were enjoying the sunshine. On the far side of the pond stood Holme Farm, amidst a group of trees clinging to the last of their autumn leaves. The barns stood right on the edge of the pond, with a tractor and cart parked in the water, all reflecting beautifully. In the far distance were the Howgills, and a dark bare tree dominated one side of the scene. I slightly changed the position of the track to help my composition.

The title of this picture just had to be 'Mucky Duck Farm', much more interesting than the farm's proper name.

Holme Farm, Cumbria (left)   *10 x 12in Oil*

One spring day, when I was once again at Holme Farm, the lady of the farm brought out some home-made cakes and tea for me whilst I was painting. It is always a pleasure to meet such nice people on my painting trips.

Autumn in Cumbria   *18 x 36in   Oil*

On an autumn sketching trip with Robin Gibbard, we left the M6 at the Sedbergh junction, one of the only motorway slip roads I know with a cattle grid.

About 2 miles down the road, we were held up by a farmer taking his sheep to lower pasture. This delay actually worked in our favour, as it allowed us time to really look at the landscape and realise what a fine subject lay before us. The old stone farmhouse caught the light and beyond was a brilliant view of the dale in sunlight after a storm. The remainder of the storm clouds were slowly disappearing behind the Howgills. The road was covered with rainwater, reflecting the rich autumn colours in the puddles.

The only aspect that spoiled the view, in my opinion, was a stark new fence, which ran towards the farm. In my painting, I substituted a stone wall, which I felt was more in keeping with the landscape.

I have since been back to the Sedbergh area many times and have always managed to find new and interesting subjects.

When this painting was reproduced as a limited edition print, it was retitled 'Into the Dales'.

Young Fisherman, River Lune, Cumbria   *12 x 16in   Oil*

Richard Thorpe from Dent acquired a short-term permit for my son, Mark, to fish the River Lune and, hopefully, catch his first trout.

They settled near a deep pool, with Richard giving instructions, 'Cast over the far side and bring the lure across to just where the current enters the deep water.'

I sat high above them, observing the expert tuition, but soon becoming distracted by the sunlight filtering through the leaves and illuminating areas deep in the cool shade. The two figures added a story to this tranquil scene, which I felt I must sketch. I worked quickly to capture the figures before they moved downstream, and I then stayed to study the subject in more detail.

The main reason I came was to watch Mark fishing, but I usually have my sketchbook with me, just in case.

Farm Near Dent, Cumbria   *18 x 36in Oil*

Dent Valley is one of my favourite areas to paint. The cottages, barns and farms nestling amongst
the hills always make interesting subjects. Low Hall Farm, Dent, is a typical example.

Low Haygarth Farm, Cautley Spout, Cumbria *18 x 24in Oil*

Clear Water, Garsdale, Cumbria   *16 x 12in Oil*

I was staying in Dent on one painting trip during an unusually hot spell. It was really too hot to paint sitting out in the sun, so I decided to go to Garsdale as there are many subjects along the tree-lined river bank, especially when the bright sunlight is filtering through the trees.

After an hour or so searching, I chose an area with a shallow pool of crystal-clear water, revealing all the rocks beneath. A waterfall fed the pool at the far end, breaking the otherwise still surface of the water with blue ripples. The sun seemed permanently to light up this area, making it the focal point of the picture.

I had walked along Clough River many times, but never noticed any trout. However, sitting here painting for several hours, I saw many large fish gliding through the clear water, only surfacing when potential food floated by.

Painting under the shade of a pine tree was perfect on such a hot day, the only drawback being that I had to wade across part of the river to reach this spot. The river bed was extremely slippery and I was relieved to get my completed wet painting back safely to the car without slipping and dropping it into the river.

Autumn Reflections, Garsdale, Cumbria   *18 x 24in Oil*